BREXIT. It's not going

Written by Michael La......
Cartoons by Anthony Smith
Book design by Irene Hoffman

Michael Lambert Publishing

This edition ©2022 Michael Lambert & Anthony Smith

First Printing
ISBN: 978-1-80068-992-3

**Subscribe to Michael Lambert's YouTube channel at
www.youtube.com/c/MichaelLambert1**

Printed in the United Kingdom

In January,1973 the United Kingdom became a member of the European Economic Community (EEC) which later became the European Union (EU), the biggest and richest trading block in the world. For over forty years everything was fine, the UK economy was doing well and everyone was happy......

However, a man called Nigel Farage, who was then leader of a party called UKIP (United Kingdom Independence Party), kept telling everyone that the UK would be much better off if we left the European Union, even though he had been a very well-paid Member of the European Parliament for twenty years.

The Prime Minister, David Cameron, was a bit afraid of Mr Farage and his friends, and some of his own backbench MPs, who also hated the EU. So, he decided to hold a referendum and ask the British public if they wanted to remain in the EU or leave.

Then Mr Farage started saying that 90 million people from Turkey would be able to come and live in the UK if we remained in the EU.

Jacob Rees-Mogg Esquire, a very silly MP who looks like an undertaker, and is famous for being very rich, kept telling poor people that if they voted to leave the EU "food, clothing and footwear" would become much cheaper.

Boris Johnson, who later became Prime Minister, drove all over the country in a big red bus with a sign on it saying that if we left the EU we would save £350 million every week, which we could spend on the NHS.

Everyone thought the UK would vote to remain in the EU, because leaving would be a catastrophic mistake which would destroy our economy and make us all poorer. However, the UK voted to leave by a tiny majority of 52% to 48%.

Then Mr Cameron resigned, leaving the mess for the new Prime Minister, Theresa May, to try to clear up. Mrs May seemed a bit confused, but in March 2017 she triggered Article 50, giving the UK just two years in which to negotiate an agreement and leave the EU.

The UK then began negotiating with the EU. The first negotiator was a man called David Davis who hardly spent any time in Brussels negotiating.

Later, Mr Davis was replaced by a man called Dominic Raab who was laughed at for telling everyone that he didn't realise the importance of the Dover to Calais route for UK-EU trade.

Mrs May then said she wanted a "strong and stable" Government and called a surprise general election. Despite the Labour leader being a scruffy old man called Jeremy Corbyn, who many people were afraid of, she did very badly and lost her majority.

Then, in order to keep her job, Mrs May had to give a lot of money to a party in Northern Ireland called the DUP (Democratic Unionist Party), who always seemed very cross and were led by a shouty lady called Arlene Foster.

Eventually, however, Mrs May had to resign because Parliament kept voting against her and then Boris Johnson became Prime Minister.
A few months later, he called a general election which he won with a majority of 80 by telling everyone that he was going to "Get Brexit Done".

In order to "Get Brexit Done", Mr Johnson asked a man called David Frost, who had no real experience of business but who was very pleased with himself and thought he was very important, to negotiate a deal with the EU.

As soon as Mr Frost had negotiated the deal, he was made a Lord and felt even more important and was even more pleased with himself. But a few months later, he realised that the deal he had negotiated was rubbish, because the shouty party in Northern Ireland didn't like it. So, Lord Frost asked the EU to re-negotiate the deal. They said 'no' which made Lord Frost look very silly.

On 1st January 2021, the UK finally left the EU and celebrated being able to 'take back control', make our own laws, stop immigrants coming to the UK, and make lots and lots of trade deals all over the world.

However, once out of the EU, thousands of businesses found they could no longer sell to the EU—the biggest and richest trade block in the world, which is just 22 miles away from England.

This was because customers in the EU did not want to pay extra, wait longer, and fill out lots of forms just to buy from the UK. So, they started buying from other countries instead.

People in the UK found that they could no longer buy from the EU, because all the new duties, extra charges, and 'red tape' made it too expensive and complicated. So, trade between the UK and the EU began to collapse.

Many British companies transferred all or part of their businesses to the EU so that they could go on trading with them. They now employ Europeans and pay taxes in the EU instead of in the UK. This has been a big 'Brexit bonus' for the EU economy.

A lady called Liz Truss, who was the International Trade Secretary, and later became the Foreign Secretary, and who loves having her photograph taken, travelled all over the world trying to get new trade deals.

After a year and a half, she had only got two new deals—one with Australia and one with New Zealand—although she did have lots of pictures of herself which she posted on Instagram and Twitter so that everyone could see how hard she was working.

The deals with Australia and New Zealand mean that, instead of buying beef and lamb from farmers in the UK, we will now be able to buy them cheaper from farmers who are 12,000 miles away. Unfortunately, however, many of our own farmers will be unable to compete and are likely to go out of business.

Having left the EU, the government now wants to join another trading block of countries based mostly around the Pacific Ocean called the CPTPP (Comprehensive and Progressive Agreement for Trans-Pacific Partnership). These countries are all an extremely long, long way away.

Mr Johnson wanted to do a big trade deal with the USA but the President, Mr Biden, said the U.S. will not do any trade deal with the UK until Mr Johnson agrees to abide by the agreement he signed with the EU called the Northern Ireland Protocol.

Fishermen, who were a very important part of the Brexit negotiations, can now fish in more British waters after Brexit. However they cannot sell their fish in the EU because of the new paperwork and delays. Many of them voted for Brexit and are now going bankrupt.

As soon as the UK left the EU on January 1st, 2021, the EU began imposing border controls in Calais and other EU ports. This means that miles of motorways in Kent have become lorry parks, whilst drivers wait for their new paperwork to be processed.

Unfortunately, almost five years after the referendum, the UK was not ready for these new border controls. Jacob Rees Mogg Esquire now says imposing checks on goods coming into the country would be an "act of self-harm" and there will be no checks before 2024. So, lorries coming into the UK at Dover are being waved through.

This means that anyone wanting to smuggle illegal goods or people into the UK can do so very easily. It also means that EU suppliers can send any poor quality or defective goods to the UK, because there are no proper checks.

Since leaving the EU, the UK now has a severe shortage of workers in many industries like farming. This means that many farmers have had to watch their crops rotting in the fields. Many will stop planting, leading to likely food shortages in future.

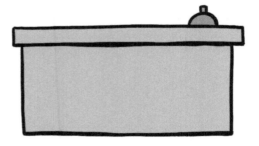

There are also shortages of workers in all sorts of other industries like healthcare, hospitality, meat and dairy, transport, social care, building and construction.

The Government is now looking all over the world in countries like India, Pakistan, the Philippines and Nigeria to find replacements for some of the EU care workers, nurses, and doctors who have gone home after Brexit.

Six years after the UK voted to leave the EU, and a year and a half after the UK finally left, Boris Johnson asked Jacob Rees Mogg Esquire to see if he could find any 'benefits from Brexit'.

He also said that one of the main benefits of having left the EU is that we will now be able to have more powerful vacuum cleaners although, if we make them, we will not be allowed to sell them in the EU.

He said that one of the main benefits of having left the EU is that we will now be able to have more powerful vacuum cleaners, although if we make them, we will not be allowed to sell them in the EU.

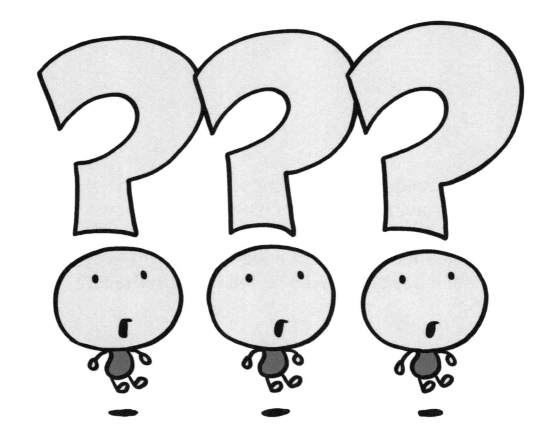

Jacob Rees Mogg Esquire also said that by not having border controls for goods coming into the country we were saving the huge cost of imposing these controls... which he seemed to think was another Brexit benefit.

As a result of Brexit, UK water companies —most of which are now owned by people in China, Australia, USA, Singapore, Germany, the UAE, Kuwait, and the Cayman Islands—can now save money by tipping raw sewage into our rivers and sea. This is because the EU can no longer stop them doing so. It also means that it is no longer safe to bathe in many of our rivers or the sea.

The Home Secretary was a woman called Priti Patel. She was a well-known bully and seemed to hate everybody, especially any foreigners who wanted to come and live in the UK, in the way that her parents did many years ago.

She only wanted to admit the "brightest and the best", and made it almost impossible for ordinary people to come and work in the UK. Because of this, more and more desperate asylum seekers have been crossing the English Channel in little boats.

This made Ms Patel extremely cross. When we were members of the EU, the French helped to stop people trying to cross the English Channel in little boats. Now that we have left the EU, and the Government keeps being rude to the EU (and especially to the French), they no longer seem to be quite so helpful.

At first Ms Patel wanted to send the asylum seekers back to France, but couldn't. Then she wanted to send them to Ascension Island, but couldn't. Then she was very happy because she planned to punish them by sending them to a country in the middle of Africa called Rwanda, and just leaving them there.

When we were members of the EU, anyone British could go and live and work in any one of twenty-seven other countries. That is no longer possible. Also UK students could spend a year in a European university. That is no longer possible.

Now we cannot even take a ham sandwich with us when travelling to the EU.

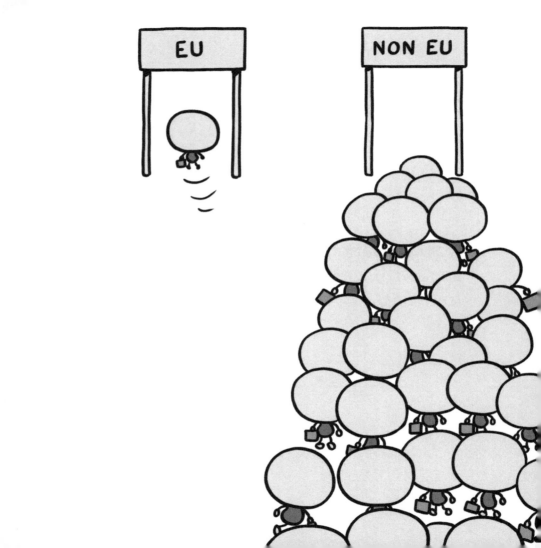

Now, when travelling to the EU, we have to wait in long queues to have our passports stamped so that we do not stay more than 90 days.

Now that we have left the EU, we have to pay telephone roaming charges again. Also, we may need travel and sickness insurance because only limited medical treatment may be available without payment.

Now that we have left the EU, we need pet passports before travelling with any cat, dog or ferret, and each has to to be microchipped.

As a member of the EU, we were involved in setting standards for the whole of the EU. Now we just have to follow whatever rules the EU imposes if we want to sell our goods to them. This is called being a 'rule taker' instead of a 'rule maker', which is what we were before.

As a member of the EU, we were part of the biggest, richest, and most successful trading block in the world. Now we have chosen to be alone, and with much reduced influence. Our exports to the EU are already 15% down, the Office for Budget Responsibility says our GDP will fall by 4% per year directly as a result of Brexit, and the OECD forecast that we will soon be the nineteenth slowest growing economy in the G20 with only Russia doing worse.

"Welcome to the Brexit, Sir".